TOUFANN

A Mauritian Fantasy

by

Dev Virahsawmy

in an English version by

Nisha and Michael Walling

This edition of *Toufann: A Mauritian Fantasy* first published in 2003 by:
Border Crossings Ltd.
13, Bankside
Enfield
EN2 8BN

Tel / Fax: +44 (0) 20 8361 2308
email: books@bordercrossings.org.uk
website: www.bordercrossings.org.uk

2nd edition 2008

A catalogue record for this book is available from the British Library.

ISBN 978-1-904718-00-0

Printed by Kent Print Management

Creolising Shakespeare: an introduction to Dev Virahsawmy's *Toufann*

by Jane Wilkinson

"Toufann": a typhoon-like storm sweeping across *The Tempest*, no longer from the Mediterranean or the Caribbean, but from Afro-Asian seas and coasts and islands, submerging the Shakespearean text in an estranging and regenerating metamorphosis. A variegated family of words connects the Indian subcontinent to China, Persia and Arabia, ancient Greece and Rome and Eastern Africa. Linked to Shakespeare, it surfaces in *Tufani*, the title of S. S. Mushi's 1969 Kiswahili translation of *The Tempest*, before breaking forth in Dev Virahsawmy's three act fantasy *Toufann*, adapted or "transcreated" from Shakespeare's play in Mauritian Creole (MC) or Morisien. Transported from Shakespeare's Atlantic-Mediterranean brew to an island in the Indian Ocean, the words and themes and characters of *The Tempest* undergo a sea-change of a new variety. Resonating in the sounds and syntax of Creole, intermixing names and identities from *Hamlet, King Lear, Othello* with others from Mauritian folklore, their bones are transformed into the coral of the hybrid social, cultural and political context of their new linguistic home.

As a translation-adaptation or transcreation, *Toufann* is the result of a transformation. But it also enacts an ongoing process of linguistic transformation and expansion: the Creole of the play is a language in progress. The very making of the language is brought to visibility, recalling the importance of language issues in *The Tempest*, only that here we are not told about but actually see the way new or foreign expressions are appropriated or imposed and others altered or discarded. The audience is present not only at the staging of Prospero's "toufann", but at its naming, witnessing the process by which the word is inserted into the play's vocabulary as it takes its place alongside the more usual "siklonn" or even supersedes it as the term to be preferred. "Toufann" is a word that has not yet been included in Creole dictionaries, but it obviously soon will be, thanks both to Virahsawmy's play and to the constant repetition or rediffusion of the term in the Hindi section of the island's multilingual weather forecasts.

All the characters in *Toufann* speak Creole, but not all speak it the same way. Not surprisingly, it is Prospero who controls - or thinks he controls - language, just as he controls - or thinks he controls - the weather, politics, perceptions and emotions current on his island. Prospero is of Indian origin, like the majority of the Mauritian population and its post-independence rulers. It is he who attributes a Hindi word to his latest brain-child, the tempest, and obliges the other characters to refer to it in the same way. In imposing the term, he is foregrounding the asymmetrical relations of power embedded in processes of language development, or, as Miranda puts it in *The Tempest*, of endowing purposes with words to make them known. But Caliban - renamed Kalibann - is no longer the object of experiments in language teaching. And Miranda-Kordelia's participation in the linguistic subplot is no longer as an ally of her father, but as the proponent of a new use of Creole. Her p.c. endeavour to eliminate the current Creole identification of cross-breed with illegitimate in its bivalent understanding of the term "batar" contributes to the revalorisation of miscegenation, but also, indirectly of Creole - no longer to be considered as a bastard offshoot of French, but a language in its own right.

Mother-tongue to many, spoken by virtually all the inhabitants of the island, Morisien is described by Virahsawmy as the "operator and symbol of cross-cultural understanding". Other languages that are or have been spoken in Mauritius include Malagasy, a Malayo-Polynesian language from Madagascar; Wolof, Fon, Bambara and other African languages; Bhojpuri, Hindi, Urdu, Marathi, Telugu and Tamil from the Indian subcontinent; various forms of Chinese; as well as English, the official language of Mauritius, spoken only by 3% of the population, and French, the language of culture, used by most of the mass-media. The characteristics of Morisien reflect the political and economic history of the island, colonized first by the French, after the failure of an initial attempt at Dutch settlement, and then the English: a history of uprootedness and displacement. The origins of the language lie in the need for communication between the Malagasy, West and East African and Indian slaves and their French masters on the sugar plantations, but also, before this, the slave traders who brought them to the island.

Soon the first generations of Creole speakers were joined by droves of indentured labourers brought over from India after the abolition of slavery, by the Chinese merchants and settlers who began to arrive later in the 19th century and by Philippinos in the 20th. Thus, much of Morisien's vocabulary comes from French, with a number of words from English, about a third as many from Indian languages, others from Malagasy and Chinese, and the vocabulary of the language - as *Toufann* shows - is in constant development, drawing not only on the input of each new group of immigrants, but on the new technologies and the plurilingual contributions of the tourist industry.

Virahsawmy is one of the major promoters of Morisien as a national language. Not only does he write in the language, but he has studied it and written about it ("Towards a Revaluation of Mauritian Creole" is the title of his dissertation at the University of Edinburgh, while in a recent article on and in Morisien he elaborates the metalanguage needed to describe it). The language issue was at the centre of the activities of the Mouvement Militant Mauricien in which Virahsawmy militated in the seventies and early eighties. Although the MMM-PSM (Parti Socialiste Militant) government (1982-3) declared Creole a national language, the result was paradoxically to activate the ethnic and cultural diversity the move was intended to oppose, culminating in the break up of the coalition and a return to the previous official language policy. It has been suggested that since there has never been a true revolutionary struggle to achieve independence in Mauritius, this has been replaced by the endeavour to assert and valorize the language on the part of the younger generations wishing to free themselves of the vestiges of colonialism. But the question is more complex. Virahsawmy sees Morisien as the language of both "decolonisation and nation-building … fast becoming the symbol of a supra-ethnic identity in a plural society". It tends to be considered the mother-tongue of the Afro-Creole community, but the majority of Mauritians, like Prospero, are of Indian descent. And in one of the three systems of orthography experimented over the years by Virahsawmy in his endeavour to promote the language, the Indian influence not only on the vocabulary but the sound of Morisien was brought to visibility by transcribing the typically Indic "tch" and "dj" phonemes. Today, emphasizing the unifying function of the language, Virahsawmy favours the orthography adopted by the Catholic Church, which has translated the liturgy into Morisien. Developing a unitary, standardized form means working against the politics of ethnic, racial or religious diversity that have gained increasing currency over the last decade, finding expression in communalistic endeavours to emphasize links to ancestral, non-Mauritian cultures in opposition to the fluid, unbounded, creolised identity-in-progress of the Mauritian present.

Translating the classics is one of Virahsawmy's strategies in his campaign in favour of Morisien. Translation, and especially the translation of Shakespeare, is a way not only "to show that MC is capable of expressing 'great thoughts'", but "To build bridges between cultures. To indicate that the establishment of MC as national language does not mean cultural isolation." Finally, translation "is also a way of sharing with others things I find beautiful" - sharing being one of the major qualities Virahsawmy attributes to creolisation. In his translations and transcreations, the logic of creolisation, or miscegenation, and sharing is carried over from language to culture. The author of original plays, poems, short stories, novellas and a novel, Virahsawmy has always attached particular importance to his translations and adaptations, including works by Brecht and the Grimms; Molière, Prévert and Saint-Exupéry; the Bible and the Maharabhata; Arnold, Blake, T. S. Eliot, Herrick, Jonson, Keats, Shelley and Yeats as well as Shakespeare. Within this project, *Toufann* plays a special role. According to its author, it is the "triumph of cultural and biological miscegenation". The "encounter of genes from different sources" is "a gain for humanity", both on the biological, cultural and linguistic level. Kalibann, Prospero's intelligent, hardworking, good-looking and good-natured mixed race computer technician and assistant turns out to be the new hero of the play. But the principle of creolisation or miscegenation affects the whole of the dramatic action, refracting on Virahsawmy's use of Shakespeare.

The characters in *Toufann* bear names from a medley of Shakespeare plays, with Miranda appearing as Kordelia, Alonso as Lerwa Lir, Sebastian as Edmon, but also Gonzalo as Poloniouss and Antonio as Yago, interacting with Prospero, Kalibann, Aryel and Ferdjinan and with the Mauritianised versions of Stefano and Trinculo, renamed Kaspalto and Dammarro. It is not just *The Tempest*, but 'Shakespeare', that is being miscegenated. Prospero's magic books and wands are replaced by computers, radars and video projections; his airy spirit by a robot. His cell is the computer control room from which he projects a virtual reality in which anything may happen, both to the fauna and geology of the island, to its inhabitants, and to the Shakespearean subtext/s and their afterlife. Yago revolts against his destiny as a stereotype of evil, invented by Shakespeare and perpetuated by the literary critics. The union between Ferdinand and Miranda is replaced by that of Kordelia and Kalibann, the future king and queen, and the homosocial coupling of Ferdjinan and Aryel, promoting not only an alternative gender orientation but full recognition of the value of emotions. Not that the solution is without its difficulties. Michael Walling's theatrical production of *Toufann* emphasized the risk of an authoritarian involution in the new leadership, while the last episode in the drama is left to the Mauritian clowns, Dammarro and Kaspalto, and their inconclusive populist rebellion against Kalibann's election. Impervious, to the end, to the lesson of generosity, care and sharing Virahsawmy attributes to miscegenation and cross-cultural understanding, they are excluded from the final reconciliation. Another limit is being underscored: although the new regime seems to have succeeded in overcoming ethnic antagonism, it is unable to confront the problem of economic injustice. Only a new text could offer a different future - but the story of the clowns' inclusion in the power structure of the country is unlikely to be written.

In *Toufann* the "Full fathom five" song has been washed away, and with it Ariel's sea-change. Yet metamorphosis and regeneration continue to pervade the text, originating in Prospero's computer control room and - despite their limits - the new alliances the play proposes. As the Wallings write in their article on *Toufann* and translation, "Kordelia's rejection of 'royal blood' in favour of 'human blood' is a plea for an inclusive politics which overturns the concept of 'batar'. Kordelia, Kalibann, Ferdjinan and Aryel all reject the doctrine of inheritance in favour of a new pluralism." Virahsawmy's version of Shakespeare's solution to political and dynastic conflict is another example of what he has called "the miscegenation vision" - the "cross-fertilization of dynamic cultural elements from Europe, Africa and Asia" already apparent in the Creole language that provides the vehicle and, surely, the major inspiration for the author's transcreations. Significantly, speaking of Creole as "the language of cohesion" in an interview with Danielle Tranquille, the metaphor he chooses for its future is "toufann": "There is a groundswell: when it surfaces, the tempest will be unleashed" ("Ena ène lam de fon, kan sela pou fer sirfas, bel toufann!").

Jane Wilkinson
Rome 2003

Jane Wilkinson is Professor of English Literature at the Università degli Studi di Napoli "L'Orientale". She is the author of *Orpheus in Africa*, *Talking with African Writers* and *Remembering "The Tempest"*.

Author's Dedication

"Pou William Shakespeare
Ek
Françoise Lionnet"

Translators' Note

Translation is almost always a process of losing the poetry. In the case of a play like Toufann, where the language issue is so basic to the writer's intentions, the translators inevitably lose even more than usual. The only way truly to appreciate the extraordinary vivacity of Virahsawmy's Renaissance-rich, remorselessly playful and punning Créole is to read it in the original. This English version is far from being a literal translation: it is a version which worked on the London stage as a way of communicating this play to an English-spreaking audience.

It is important to understand the ethnic composition of the cast. Prospero and his family are of Indian origin, like the politically dominant group in contemporary Mauritius. King Lir and his family are white. Kaspalto and (in our production) the Sailor are black. Dammarro is Indian, and Kalibann is mixed race (white and black African).

Kaspalto and Dammarro are the folkloric clowns of Mauritian culture. Kaspalto is an African drunkard, and Dammarro an Indian junkie. In Mauritian Creole, "Kas-palto" means "turncoat". In Hindi, "Damm" means "take a breath" or "get a kick"; "marro" means "kill it" or "stifle it". Kaspalto is also the name for a very cheap brand of wine.

Nisha & Michael Walling

This version of *Toufann* was originally presented by Border Crossings at the Africa Centre, London, in 1999.

Cast (in order of appearance)

Sailor	*Jason Mayne*
Poloniouss (The King's advisor)	*Charles Phillips*
Kordelia (Prospero's daughter)	*Catherine Mobley*
Prospero	*Shaun Chawdhary*
Kalibann	*Chris Ryman*
Aryel	*Aaron Ashton*
King Lir	*John Pine*
Edmon (King Lir's brother)	*Martin Head*
Yago (Prospero's brother)	*Hari Sajjan*
Ferdjinan (King Lir's son)	*Dominic Cazenove*
Kaspalto	*Zandy Lekau*
Dammarro	*Pasha*
The Sega Dancer	*Connie Poonoosamy*
Directed by	Michael Walling
Designed by	Martin McLeod
Lighting by	Matthew Attwood
Video by	David Wheeler
Costumes by	Nisha Walling
Assistant Director	Alistair Bamford
Production Manager	Simon Rhodes
Stage Manager	Jo Crowley
Lighting Assistant	Matt Haskins

The production was sponsored by Air Mauritius

ACT 1. Scene 1.

(A cyclone. Wind, rain, lightning, thunder. A modern ship is stuck in the cyclone.)

SAILOR: Fuck off out of the way, you idiot! You're stopping me working!

POLONIOUSS: Now listen, my man! Do you know who you're talking to? I'm the King's advisor. If I -

SAILOR: I don't give a toss! Go and advise the King to get ready for swimming! I want you out of here. Get into your cabin and say your prayers.

POLONIOUSS: Whatever happens - you are done for. If this ship sinks, you're done for. And if we're saved, then I'll see to it you're really done for!

SAILOR: Captain! Looks like there's something right in front of us - Looks like an island -

KING LIR: (from offstage) Are you mad? There's nothing on the map. There's nothing on the radar either.

SAILOR: All the same, Captain... We're heading straight for it.

POLONIOUSS: You're out of your mind, my friend. Where's this island that's supposed to be straight ahead?

SAILOR: You blind old git!

POLONIOUSS: Look out, chum. Don't overstep the mark.

KING LIR: (from offstage) Captain, something's not normal. Turn around, change course - too late! God pardon my sin!

(Chaos)

ACT 1. Scene 2.

(In Prospero's control room. Kordelia and Prospero.)

KORDELIA: Dad! Why did you turn off the monitors? Didn't you see the ship? It's heading straight for us. It'll crash on the reef.

PROSPERO: Keep quiet! I know what I'm doing.... My time has come.

KORDELIA: Your time? Hundreds of people are about to die, and you sit still and watch, just because of your time! What time?

PROSPERO: Kordelia, don't question me. Be re-assured. Not so much as a fly will be hurt. It's all under control. Their lives are in my hands... Just watch me!

KORDELIA: Mr. Prospero, when you talk like this, it scares me. You behave as if you wanted to take the place of God.

PROSPERO: Well, daughter, you're very close! Soon you will understand everything. Send for Aryel! Tell him to be quick! Don't stand there like you've been mummified - go and tell Aryel to come here quickly.

(Kordelia goes out, and Prospero speaks to himself.)

Twenty[1] years of patience, twenty years of work, twenty years of research. Today, I am the one who controls Toufann[2], I control the tempest, I am the one who decides, I am the one who controls everything. King Lir, you profited from my weakness, you abandoned myself and my daughter to the cyclone in nothing but a nutshell of a boat, sending us to be swallowed up by the rain and wind. You wanted to destroy me. Well, King Lir, today the wheel has come full circle. We will see now how you face my Toufann....

(calls off)

Kalibann! Kalibann, you worthless... KA-LI-BANN! Have you gone deaf?

(Kalibann enters. He is a young man, around 25, of mixed race. He is good-looking, intelligent and hard-working.)

KALIBANN: Sir, do you need me?

PROSPERO: If I call you, then I need you! Did you do what I told you?

KALIBANN: Yes sir. But -

PROSPERO: But what? You're not here to ask questions - you're here to carry out my orders. Understood?

---

1   Translators' Note: Dev Virahsawmy wrote TOUFANN in 1991. This was twenty-three years after Mauritius became an independent country within the Commonwealth. One year later, in 1992, Mauritius became an Republic.
2   The word Toufann is originally a Hindi word for hurricane (or cyclone, as they are known in Mauritius). It entered Mauritian Creole through the language of Bhojpuri, which is spoken by many Mauritian people of Bihari descent.

KALIBANN: Mr. Prospero!

PROSPERO: What now?

KALIBANN: Don't you think we should let them go?

PROSPERO: Who are you to go advising me? Speak when you're spoken to. Don't forget what I saved you from. You and your mother were starving to death when I came here...And don't forget the promise your mother made. That you would work with me, for me, obeying me for as long as I want. Right!

KALIBANN: Yes sir.

PROSPERO: Have you done a checklist?

KALIBANN: Here.

PROSPERO: Good. Let me see. You won't have thought of everything.... No, it's... Right. Have you set up?

KALIBANN: Yes sir. It's all ready for the first projection. Equipment adjusted.

(Kordelia and Aryel enter. Aryel is a blonde giant with blue eyes.)

PROSPERO: Aryel, have you checked everything? Are you satisfied?

ARYEL: AOK, captain. Your wish is my command.

PROSPERO: Any problems?

ARYEL: Captain, if something's difficult I do it instantly. Things that are impossible take me a little longer.

PROSPERO: No need to blow your own trumpet. Now, you two get out for a bit - I've something to say to Kordelia in private.

(Kalibann and Aryel exit. At the door, Kalibann moves aside, letting Aryel leave first.)

                 Now Kordelia, sit here and pay attention.

KORDELIA: Is there something the matter, Dad?

PROSPERO: A story from long ago. I've had to wait my time to let you into the know.

KORDELIA: You keep on talking about "your time" - what do you mean?

PROSPERO: Just listen, child. Listen. Do you remember how and when we came here? And the state we were in?

KORDELIA: Only vaguely. I remember a hut. A sailing boat with a torn sail. Kalibann. His mother - Auntie Bangoya.

PROSPERO:	You were too small. The time's come for me to tell you everything. Kordelia - you weren't born here. You were born in a palace - and your mother was the most beautiful woman who ever drew breath. For myself, I was a powerful king - respected. All the countries round about were jealous of my kingdom, because in my country people were happy. Things couldn't have been better. A good government, an efficient workforce. How can I explain? I didn't have a care in the world. I spent my time reading and writing - I didn't even notice that I was spending more time in my library than at Government House.... A bit at a time, I handed over all my power to the Prime Minister. My brother. An honest man, hard-working, intelligent... too intelligent. Cunning. Little by little, he managed to get absolute power for himself. Without me even noticing, he gets rid of ministers one after the other - putting in his men everywhere, police, army, the law.... everywhere you go, nothing but his men. And so, bit by bit, he got all the power. It's meant to be basic to any democracy that you separate the executive from the legislature! Not him.....
KORDELIA:	Come on, Dad, what happened then?
PROSPERO:	All right, my darling - don't rush me! He's a snake! I did everything for him. He was an unknown, a complete nobody. And I was fool enough to trust him. Yago - that's his name - sees that I'm out of the way, and decides to make a pact with our country's oldest enemies! And what was I up to? I'm in the library, with my head in my books, in the lab, doing the research....
KORDELIA:	What research?
PROSPERO:	I'll come to that. But Yago - this pig called Yago joins forces with Prince Edmon, King Lir's brother, and the three of them hatched their plot. One morning, a troop of soldiers attacked my palace. Just like today, there was a huge cyclone -wind, rain, lightning, thunder.... The soldiers marched into the palace and took me prisoner. When they tried to get into your nursery.... You were only a new-born baby!.... Your mother tried to stop them. They killed her.
KORDELIA:	Oh God.
PROSPERO:	They took the two of us and put us in a boat. Boat! Nothing but a nutshell. All they let me take was a couple of books. That was thanks to Poloniouss's kindness. Poor Poloniouss. Not a bad man, but God does he talk! Anyway, he was able to give us ome food and clothes, secretly. For a whole week, maybe even longer, we sailed rocking and shaking through the storm and the burning sun, until we reached this island. A small inhabited island, very close to hell. There was a hut, where Bangoya was living with her half-bred batar.[3]
KORDELIA:	Batar?
PROSPERO:	You know who I mean - Kalibann. Bangoya was a negress: a slave. Her owner was a pirate. He got her pregnant, then abandoned her on our island.
KORDELIA:	Sad.

---

3   Translator's note: in Mauritian Creole, the word "batar" can mean both "bastard" and "person of mixed race". Both usages are applied to Kalibann throughout the play.

PROSPERO:	Sad? I'd call it worrying. That Kalibann has a very disturbing genetic make-up. It didn't take me long to change the way of life on this island. I've used all my knowledge to turn it into a little paradise for you, for myself, and everyone who obeys me. It's not as if we were lacking in resources. Nature is very generous. And science has allowed me to take charge of nature, and realise my plan. Twenty years on, day by day, I can test out my theories.
KORDELIA:	And Aryel?
PROSPERO:	What about Aryel?
KORDELIA:	How did he get here?
PROSPERO:	I am myself both his father and mother.
KORDELIA:	Now Dad - don't try to tell me you're some sort of hermaphrodite....
PROSPERO:	More than that! I'm his God - I created him. He is the child of my power, my cience, my technology: the creature of my competence. He's a robot who is not a robot, a human who is not human. And, whenever I wanted, I could make thousands more just like him.
KORDELIA:	It's as if your power was supernatural....
PROSPERO:	They made use of a storm for my torture. Today I have made Toufann as the instrument of my revenge. My hot sauce, my rare pickle.
KORDELIA:	It sounds so dangerous - the slightest slip, and things could get out of control, and then -
PROSPERO:	Don't be afraid. There won't be any slips. I'm completely in control. Not one of them has felt even the slightest scratch. I had to frighten them, to make them understand what they'd done. To make them repentant. That's all.
KORDELIA:	You talk as if you really were God, and that does frighten me. It wasn't just your enemies who were on the ship -there were innocent people too.
PROSPERO:	Why do you say "were"? They are still with us! And what a sight they are - thinking they've just seen a miracle!
KORDELIA:	Where are they?
PROSPERO:	In the hallucination of a harbour which I've created in the middle of the island[4]. They thought they would crash on the cliffs, but the mountain opened, and a canal carried them to a lake at the island's heart, where their ship is becalmed and safe. They think they're dreaming. The mountain's closed again, the canal has disappeared. Once the account is settled, they can come out, and sail back to the ocean. Do you see? They're safe - only they don't know it. Clear?

4   In Mauritius, there is a lake called Grand Bassin (Cr: basen). Early immigrants, arriving from India, poured Ganga water into the lake, which is now regarded as a Mauritian version of the sacred river from their ancestral home. Prospero's reference to "the hallucination of a harbour" clearly has resonances here.

KORDELIA: No.

PROSPERO: You will understand: later.

ACT 1. Scene 3.

(On the ship. King Lir and Poloniouss.)

POLONIOUSS:	Don't be so down-hearted, Your Majesty. The storm didn't hurt a fly. The Captain says there's no damage to the ship. We've only one real problem: there doesn't seem to be any way out. We're surrounded by mountains. How we got here is beyond me.
KING LIR:	I'm quite convinced we're all dead. This place is Purgatory. We're waiting for the Last Judgement.
POLONIOUSS:	If I may say so, Your Majesty, that's a bit pessimistic. What's the problem? If this really is Purgatory, it strikes me that Purgatory is better than Paradise.
KING LIR:	How would you know?
POLONIOUSS:	I'm using my imagination.
KING LIR:	This is your problem, Poloniouss. You're always using your imagination. It's not a good idea for a politician.
POLONIOUSS:	To my mind, Your majesty, imagination is a way of thinking. You start from an hypothesis, and then -
KING LIR:	Poloniouss, I'm really not in the mood for a lecture on language, truth and logic! (Pause) I don't know why, but I keep seeing something... It comes and goes, swirling in my mind...
POLONIOUSS:	What is it?
KING LIR:	A little boat. In a cyclone.
POLONIOUSS:	That's very strange. I've been seeing the same thing.

(Enter Yago and Edmon)

EDMON:	Lir!
KING LIR:	Yes, Edmon.
EDMON:	Yago and I have been off the ship for a bit, having a look round. There's no problem with stuff to eat and drink - Nature's been pretty kind to this place. The only real problem is this: there's absolutely no way of getting back to the sea. It's like our ship's flown across the island, and landed on this mini-lake thing. Can't even call it a lake, can you? It's more like a pond. Just about big enough for the ship to float in. Gentlemen, we are in an impossible predicament. We are trapped on a pond in the middle of a deserted island in the middle of nowhere.
YAGO:	Deserted, yes. I'd say we were probably the first people ever to set foot here. I propose we publish a decree which declares this island to be an official part of your

Empire, and naming myself as the Prime Minister.

KING LIR: Yago, I can't honestly feel that political manoeuvring is a priority issue at the moment! Isn't it more important simply to find a way out of here?

EDMON: Come on Lir: I think Yago's talking a lot of sense. We need to get this island organised. Our ship should take on the role of Government House. I'm quite sure there are gold and diamond deposits. We've got a workforce ready-made: turn the sailors into miners.

KING LIR: What are we going to do with gold and diamonds when we have lost our liberty?

POLONIOUSS: Your Majesty, this is an ideal opportunity to experiment with various models of government. You remember my theories regarding autocracy...

YAGO: He's off again.

EDMON: Verbal diarrhoea.

KING LIR: What is happening to all of you, for God's sake? This is no time for theorising! All I want to know is how to get out of this trap.

(Enter sailor)[5]

SAILOR: Majesty. Is Prince Ferdjinan here?

KING LIR: No. Didn't he go with you to explore the island?

SAILOR: Yes, majesty, we were together.... But after a while we realised he wasn't with us any more. He'd just vanished. We thought he'd probably come back to the ship. We've looked everywhere, but there's no sign of him. (Pause) Majesty, there's a strange feeling about this place. We heard voices. In the sky, from the trees, in the water. All around us. It felt like they were laughing. With a sort of ugly mischief. Majesty - I'm afraid something horrible may have happened.

KING LIR: Ferdjinan! My Hell starts here.

POLONIOUSS: You mustn't think like that. Ferdjinan's able to look after himself. Perhaps he's exploring some cave he's found, or something. Perhaps he's met tribal people in the   mountains. Perhaps -

YAGO: Perhaps he's playing hide and seek with the monkeys. Perhaps, perhaps, perhaps.

POLONIOUSS: Instead of comforting somebody in pain -

EDMON: Comfort? Consolation? Cobblers!

KING LIR: My son. My heir.

POLONIOUSS: Majesty! Often when things seem quite hopeless, they actually turn out for the best.

---

5   In the original, three soldiers enter here. We've amalgamated them into the sailor in the interests of a more economical cast size.

KING LIR:	No, Poloniouss. Sins have to be paid for - even here on earth. Remember that little boat in the cyclone? I understand it now. This is God's punishment for the worst of my crimes. I showed no pity - not for a poor, innocent baby. Now God has put me into Purgatory so that I too can feel the suffering of a father. May Prospero forgive me!
YAGO:	Prospero? What's Prospero got to do with it?
EDMON:	*(aside to Yago)* He's cracking up.
YAGO:	*(aside to Edmon)* All the better for you. Now's your moment. Keep a tight grip.
POLONIOUSS:	Lir, my King...
KING LIR:	No Poloniouss. Don't try to comfort me. I have to pay. Let me pay.

ACT 1. Scene 4.

(In Prospero's control-room. Prospero and Kordelia.)

PROSPERO: No, Kordelia, don't go. Stay here. I've something important to show you.

KORDELIA: Let me go and see them. They've suffered enough - let me go and calm them down.

PROSPERO: It's still too soon. You can go and see them when the time is right. At the moment they're still infected with evil.

(Aryel enters. With him is Ferdjinan, who is hypnotised.)

ARYEL: Captain, this is a remarkable young man.

PROSPERO: Really?

ARYEL: In his place, anybody else would have cracked. Not him. He responds so instinctively to beauty: the music from the heavens, the flowers and animals of the island. As if this was all normal for him. I played my flute, and he followed me like an artist following his muse.

PROSPERO: Really.

ARYEL: Of course, I don't understand human emotion; but there's something about the expression on his face...

PROSPERO: He's still hypnotised, that's all. Now, Kordelia, what do you think?

KORDELIA: About what?

PROSPERO: Well, you're twenty now - it's about time we got you married, isn't it?

KORDELIA: Who to?

PROSPERO: What about him?

KORDELIA: Him? Who is he?

PROSPERO: Prince Ferdjinan. He's King Lir's son.

KORDELIA: Hang on. You're asking me to marry the son of your enemy?

PROSPERO: Of course! That way we get revenge. You marry Ferdjinan - King Lir gets deposed - you're the Queen!

KORDELIA: What if I don't agree?

PROSPERO: You simply have to. You can't throw a spanner in the works today.

KORDELIA: Why's he catatonic?

PROSPERO: Aryel's hypnotised him. Let's bring him round.

(Prospero claps his hands, and Ferdjinan wakes up.)

FERDJINAN: What happened? Where am I?

PROSPERO: Aryel! Watch carefully.

FERDJINAN: Excuse me, Miss - may I ask who you are?

PROSPERO: See, Aryel - he doesn't talk to you or me!

ARYEL: I'm invisible, captain.

FERDJINAN: Please do tell me, Miss. Are you a dream, or are you as real as myself?

PROSPERO: Kordelia, I don't want you talking to him! Look at him; you can see which family
              he comes from! He no sooner sees a skirt, but he's wanting to lift it up! Aryel, slam
              him in the cooler!

KORDELIA: You're over-reacting! What's he supposed to have done?

PROSPERO: Don't argue! Lock him up.

FERDJINAN: Sir, please explain -

PROSPERO: I'm the one who asks for explanations!

FERDJINAN: I'm treating you with courtesy! Miss, please tell him I don't mean any harm. I don't
              even know where I am... whether this is really happening, or just some awful
              nightmare. The strangest things keep happening. First, our ship hits the cyclone -

PROSPERO: Toufann!

FERDJINAN: Pardon?

PROSPERO: Not cyclone, Toufann.

FERDJINAN: Same thing, isn't it? Anyway, by some miracle we survived it. The ship ended up
              on a landlocked pond with mountains all round. I left the ship with some of the
              sailors; but suddenly I found I was all alone. I heard fantastic music, and I saw what
              I can only call a vision of the sublime. I followed where the music led me... and it
              led me to you.

KORDELIA: You ought to know -

PROSPERO: Shut up, Kordelia! Aryel - throw him into the darkest prison; the most humid, the
              most rat-infested.

(Aryel seizes Ferdjinan, who does not understand what is happening because he can't see Aryel. They exit.)

KORDELIA: Why did you do that?

PROSPERO: His father didn't hesitate to throw us into a storm -

KORDELIA: His father, not him!

PROSPERO: Tell me once and for all - will you marry him or not?

KORDELIA: I've not made up my mind yet!

PROSPERO: You'd better be quick! There's not much time left. By sunset, everything must be accomplished.

ACT 1. Scene 5.

(On board King Lir's ship. Kaspalto and Dammarro.)

KASPALTO: Wild, man! You pluck a coconut, you crack it open, you drink it - what d'ya find? Whisky! It's Paradise, man!

DAMMARRO: Now I know why you are bringing so big a bunch.

KASPALTO: Breakfast, lunch, dinner. Then in the morning, I'm finding a whole bunch more. Whacha doing, man?

DAMMARRO: I am rolling myself a nice big joint.

KASPALTO: You kidding, Dammarro? You can't get weed here too?

DAMMARRO: Kaspalto, I am telling you - you get this stuff, no problem. There is a whole field out there, my friend. We're talking big business here. So far, I have two sacks full. Tomorrow, I am harvesting again. Today - relaxation! Dam marro dam! Hare Krishna, hare Ram! Eh, Kaspalto - you want a drag?

KASPALTO: No way, man! Whisky's the only thing for me.... Say, Dammarro - why d'ya think everybody's looking for, like, a way out? You know - if the brothers just knew the wild life we're leading - cheers! - they'd be fighting so as they could get shipwrecked too. Don't come rescuing me, man! I wants to stay here always, for ever and ever, Amen! Fancy a swig, Dammarro?

DAMMARRO: Niet! I'm walking on the ceiling.... Just let me dream. Beauty for the eye and ear.... Dam marro dam....

(Edmon and Yago enter.)

EDMON: Hey, Kaspalto, Dammarro! What are you two up to?

KASPALTO: Mr. Edmon, Mr. Yago - you want a swig?

YAGO: Coconut milk! I don't mind if I do.

KASPALTO: Watch your throat, man.

YAGO: Bloody hell! What have you put in it?

KASPALTO: I've not put nothing in it, Mr. Yago. That's nature you're tasting. Just pluck it off the tree.... Ain't that right, Dammarro?

DAMMARRO: Just pluck it off the tree.... Dam marro dam! No problem!

YAGO: *(to Kaspalto)* Can you show me where you found this?

KASPALTO: Everywhere! Wherever you look and wherever you go, there's the call of the coconut. I'm telling you, Boss - the priests are right. Paradise is.... heavenly. Praise the Lord! *(He kisses the coconut.)* Kiss the Bible!

EDMON: Yago, let's go. I have something serious to discuss with you.

(Yago and Edmon go out.)

DAMMARRO: Kaspalto - are you not scare they may be spilling the beans?

(There is sublime music playing....)

KASPALTO: No man! Don't you go worrying. Mr. Yago, Mr. Edmon, they're good guys! Don't go bothering them, they won't go bothering you. *(He yawns.)* Hey man! You can worry without my help: I'm going to sleep. *(He sleeps.)*

DAMMARRO: Hey - wake up! We need to harvest some more treasure! Get up you stupid asshole! Hum.... My eyes are feeling very heav.... mm. (He sleeps.)

(Aryel enters. He changes their clothes. Kaspalto is dressed up as Yago, and Dammarro like Edmon. He does a magic trick, speaks in their ears, then disappears. They wake up.)

KASPALTO: Dammarro, get up! Didn't you hear me? Get up!

DAMMARRO: Call me by my name. Who is this Dammarro fellow? You know damn well I am called Edmon. Why are you dressed up like that, Kaspalto?

KASPALTO: Dressed up! Bullshit, man! And it's Yago to you!

DAMMARRO: A thousand apologies, your honour. Please do follow me. I have something serious to discuss with you. Dam marro dam.

(They leave.)

ACT 1. Scene 6.

(In the dungeon. Ferdjinan and Kordelia.)

FERDJINAN: I just don't understand! What am I supposed to have done to your father? He puts me in prison. AND I get lifted up, pulled around, mauled about, immobilised - all by some invisible force. Will you please explain what's going on!

KORDELIA: Calm down! It will all make sense soon.... My father said I shouldn't tell you anything. I shouldn't really even be here. If it wasn't for Kalibann's help -

FERDJINAN: Kalibann?

KORDELIA: He's my father's..... assistant. He knows all the secrets. Like the passages where the cameras can't spy on us. He's even disconnected the dungeon surveillance camera for a bit...

FERDJINAN: Why?

KORDELIA: Because I asked him to. (Pause.) I know you've done nothing wrong. He's punishing you for something your father did.

FERDJINAN: My father?

KORDELIA: King Lir, right?

FERDJINAN: Yes.

KORDELIA: Have you heard about King Prospero?

FERDJINAN: Vaguely. He attempted some sort of coup. It failed. Now he lives in exile.

KORDELIA: And what about his daughter?

FERDJINAN: I didn't know he had one.

KORDELIA: You're talking to her.

(Beat)

KORDELIA: History's a pretty subjective thing, Ferdjinan. Your father tells you Prospero led a failed coup: my father says Lir and Yago conspired to destroy him.... Now he has a plan...

(Kalibann comes in.)

KALIBANN: Kordi! Hurry up. Your father might see.

KORDELIA: Won't be long, Kal. Have you met Prince Ferdjinan?

KALIBANN: No.

FERDJINAN:	Morning. *(To Kordelia.)* So what's this plan?
KALIBANN:	Plan?
KORDELIA:	*(To Kalibann.)* It's a different issue. I'll tell you later. You can go and replug the camera - I've just a couple more things to tell Ferdjinan.
KALIBANN:	Careful, then, Kordi. You've only got sixty seconds. Hurry up. *(He goes out.)*
KORDELIA:	OK, listen carefully. My father is a scientific genius. He has a lot of power - over nature and over people. He can start a cyclone - this thing he calls Toufann. He can project images into the environment, and people believe them. Your ship is imprisoned in a virtual reality which he has constructed. And it's all about revenge.
FERDJINAN:	Revenge?
KORDELIA:	Twenty years ago your father, your uncle and my uncle deposed him. Now he wants to do the same to them. He'll get all their power in his hands and create a massive new empire. And you and me - we're only pawns in the game.
FERDJINAN:	You and me?
KORDELIA:	I've got to be quick - the camera will be back on soon. He wants to make me queen through you.
FERDJINAN:	Does that mean what I think it does?
KORDELIA:	He wants us to get married.
FERDJINAN:	Oh no - oh no....
KORDELIA:	Some problem?
FERDJINAN:	Well.... no offence, but..... you understand...
KORDELIA:	Then get thinking! We've got to find a way around this. I have to go now. I'll be in touch again.

(She goes.)

| FERDJINAN: | My dream is turning into a nightmare..... Where's this hidden camera? Can't see a thing in this pit! I don't want to be King anyway - Kordelia can have my place! But I will not let them force me to marry. No way. I can't make a life with a woman - that's not who I am. Oh God... What's his name? Kabi... no - Kila.... Kalibann! Perhaps he can help. Kalibann! I'm trapped - I'm trapped. This is hell. Kalibann! |

ACT 1. Scene 7.

(In Prospero's control-room. All the screens are alight. From here Prospero controls everything. He seems satisfied. He is standing in front of a big keyboard, full of switches and buttons.)

PROSPERO: Tick: rainfall. Tock: sunrise. Time to shock them a bit. How about a volcanic eruption? No - too extreme. I know; a dinosaur. Here we go! Ha-ha! Just watch them run! Lir, where are you? Ah - here. Feeling sorry for yourself. Good: it's high time I gave you a taste of your own medicine.

(Aryel enters.)

Aryel - what's up? Everything going well?

ARYEL: I think so. Prince Ferdjinan is biting his nails in prison. And his father is in an even worse toufann. He's not eating or drinking; his eyes are full of tears. It's sad, Captain.

PROSPERO: Sad?

ARYEL: Captain, I don't understand human emotion - this isn't a feature in my make-up - but when I look at the poor miserable king in his pitiful condition, it makes me feel..... peculiar.

PROSPERO: Aryel, you're not programmed to feel peculiar. Your function is logical, objective reasoning.

ARYEL: Yes, Captain.

PROSPERO: Now, we have to be especially careful of Yago and Edmon. Those two make trouble everywhere they go.

ARYEL: Captain, I've used my initiative for a little mischief of my own.

PROSPERO: What have you done?

ARYEL: Don't be angry, Captain. You see, I overheard Yago and Edmon hatching some plot, and I thought I could see a way of stirring things up even more. Do you know Kaspalto and Dammarro?

PROSPERO: No, who are they?

ARYEL: A right pair of air-heads. One alcoholic, one junkie.

PROSPERO: Well, what about them?

ARYEL: I hope this wasn't a mistake. I hypnotised and disguised them, so that one thinks he's Yago, and the other Edmon. They present what you might call an alternative image of royalty.

PROSPERO: Brilliant! Here's what we should do next. Get them back to the ship, make yourself invisible and use them to create chaos. You've got carte blanche for total confusion. OK? Is there something else? Speak up - don't be scared.

ARYEL: Can I make myself visible to Prince Ferdjinan?

PROSPERO: Why?

ARYEL: Because I want to console him.

PROSPERO: Your vocabulary's expanding! Console him?

ARYEL: Captain, if I can get his sympathy, he might be very useful to us.

PROSPERO: If you think so. Go and see to the air-heads first. *(Aryel exits.)* He's getting emotional. That's not in the plan. Emotion can really snarl things up. A machine talking like a human ..... Careful, Prospero. You've been ruined by emotion in your time. It's a weakness on which malice thrives. Emotion.... a plague which eats away at the mind. A wave which could easily wash away my whole plan. *(Enter Kordelia.)* Yes, Kordelia?

KORDELIA: Oh - it's you.

PROSPERO: Are you looking for something?

KORDELIA: I thought Kalibann was here.

PROSPERO: No.

KORDELIA: It's no problem.

PROSPERO: Can I help?

KORDELIA: No, it's nothing. It's just that my computer printer's not working... There's no hurry - it can wait.

PROSPERO: Have you thought about my proposal?

KORDELIA: It's hard to decide.

PROSPERO: Why?

KORDELIA: You want me to decide whether to marry a man who you've put in prison, and whom I can't even see.

PROSPERO: So what's the problem?

KORDELIA: Well - you have to know somebody before you can choose them, and to know somebody you have to meet them. And I've not met him.

PROSPERO: If that's all, why not go and meet him?

KORDELIA: Where?

PROSPERO: In the prison -

KORDELIA: Dad!

PROSPERO: OK! I'll have him sent to your apartment. Wait for Aryel - I've just sent him to do something else.

(Pause)

KORDELIA: How are the prisoners getting on?

PROSPERO: Haven't you been watching on the monitors? They're like fish out of water.

KORDELIA: People in a storm.

PROSPERO: Exactly! People caught in my Toufann. Confused, bewildered - paralysed in the mind. Fear. Panic. Trauma.

KORDELIA: And that makes you happy?

PROSPERO: Kordelia - you have no idea of what I'm feeling. I've been working for twenty years. Twenty years I've been waiting...

KORDELIA: You're right - I don't understand.

PROSPERO: You will understand. When it's finished. When the final curtain falls. Oh - it's too soon to explain now. It's like a play. I've written it, and now I'm directing it scene by scene. All the actors have to do is perform the way I want them to.

KORDELIA: And if an actor wants to improvise -

PROSPERO: I won't allow it.

KORDELIA: - or to rewrite a scene?

PROSPERO: Don't taunt me! Trust your father, Kordelia. It's for you I'm doing all this, you know - for your happiness. For twenty years all my work and care has been that what happened to me should never happen to you.

KORDELIA: Dad. I adore you - you know I do - but when you play at God, you frighten me.

PROSPERO: I'm not playing at God. I'm putting right God's mistakes. Helping him out a bit - fulfilling his work, perhaps.

KORDELIA: But God made people free. You're trying to control them.

PROSPERO: Yes! If people would only follow the destiny I've given them, the world would be a paradise.

KORDELIA: We'll see about that. Won't we?

PROSPERO: Oh yes, my love. We certainly will. Good! Enough talk. Time to start the second phase of the programme.

KORDELIA: How many phases are there going to be?

PROSPERO: Three. Like in a modern play.

*

ACT 2. Scene 1.

(The ship. King Lir, Poloniouss, the Sailor.)

POLONIOUSS: If you keep dwelling on your own misfortunes, you'll only get depressed. And depression paralyses the mind. It leaves you incapable of doing what leaders - Kings - have to do. Don't forget that a King remains a king whatever the circumstances. It's your duty to keep up morale amongst your subjects. Besides - every cloud has a silver lining, you know. Perhaps none of us are suffering a real calamity - not even you.

KING LIR: A real calamity? My son, my only son,the heir to the throne and the most important person in my life has disappeared, vanished completely; I find myself a prisoner in all but name; my ship is stranded on a pond; my country is without a government; nobody knows how to get back to the sea - and you dare to tell me that it isn't a real calamity?

POLONIOUSS: Keep your head! If we can only work out why these things are happening to us, then perhaps -

KING LIR: Perhaps, perhaps, perhaps.... Poloniouss, sometimes I think your jaw gets too much exercise.

POLONIOUSS: Yes, Your Majesty - I just wanted to point out that we mustn't get too down-hearted.

SAILOR: Mr. Poloniouss is right, Your Majesty. The ship's perfectly sea-worthy. No mechanical problems, plenty of fuel. The only problem -

KING LIR: The only problem is that there's no sea to sail on! I'm sick of the lot of you. Incompetent! What we need is Prospero. He could have got us out of this mess. He didn't waste time with all this politicking; he wasn't lining his own pocket or looking after his own skin. He didn't even care about party loyalties or any of that rubbish.[6] He just studied science - for its own sake. If he'd been here, he would have known what to do. I should have made him my closest ally, not thrown him to one side. Yago and Edmon have been the ruin of me.

POLONIOUSS: I hate to say I told you so....

KING LIR: If you could see that I was losing my grip, why didn't you say so?

POLONIOUSS: If you remember, sir, I did try to make you understand. But you were always so furious when I disagreed with you, that I preferred to stay silent.

KING LIR: So you accept that you are to blame!

POLONIOUSS: Yes, Your Majesty.

---

6   In the original Creole, King Lir is referring here to a specific political speech, in which Harish Boodhoo likened the various ethnic groups in Mauritius to monkeys defending their mountains from one another

KING LIR:	Then why are you still rattling on?
POLONIOUSS:	Let's just forget the past. Wipe it from our memories.
KING LIR:	I can't forget. Because of them I went against my better judgement, and did something so wrong... If I ever get my power back then I shall find Prospero, and make him my ally - and then they will be the ones who get cast adrift! Perhaps exile might teach them a little humanity. They were the ones who tricked me - the flies who laid their filthy eggs inside my skull - and now it's crawling with maggots! Oh, Ferdjinan... And to think that the whole point of this voyage was so that you could marry some wretched millionaire princess. All to increase and consolidate our worldly power. Well, now my plans are wrecked. Shipwrecked in a pond. I am a shark in a miniature aquarium.
SAILOR:	Your Majesty! Prince Edmon and Yago are heading this way. They are singing as they walk. I think they must be sea-sick or something.
POLONIOUSS:	Either that or they're....
KING LIR:	Drunk! Instead of tackling our problems they decide to let their hair down! God - if there is any justice....

(Enter Kaspalto and Dammarro disguised as Yago and Edmon. Aryel follows them, invisible.)

POLONIOUSS:	Yago, is this really an appropriate way to behave?
KASPALTO:	*(singing)* Tcharli O, Tcharli O. Aret bwar, aret bwar, djiven banann. Dan djiven banann ena bebet sizo....[7]
KING LIR:	Yago, if you don't listen to me....
KASPALTO:	*(singing)* Tchi Mimi lav sa ver la Lav sa ver la Met zafer la, koko.
KING LIR:	Edmon, are you responsible for this?
POLONIOUSS:	Come on, Edmon, look sharp. The King's talking to you!
DAMMARRO:	*(singing)* Lucy in the sky with diamonds, Lucy in the sky with diamonds....
KING LIR:	Is this some sort of secret code?[8]
POLONIOUSS:	Prince Edmon, are you feeling all right? Come with me to your cabin, and you can have a little rest. Help me, somebody!

---

7   Kaspalto's songs are popular Creole melodies. We've left them in the original language, partly because the sense doesn't matter so much as their folk quality, but also because the scene is intended to have the quality of linguistic confusion. In the original, this gets introduced through Dammarro's quotation of the Beatles.

8   In the Creole, King Lir refers here to "Madame Sere", or Gypsy Langauge; the Mauritian name for the game of putting "eg" in front of every vowel sound.

DAMMARRO:	(singing) Picture yourself in a boat in a basen[9],
	With plasticine trees and a marmalade sky,
	Newspaper taxis with your heads in the cloud,
	A girl with kaleidoscope eyes.
	Lucy in the sky with diamonds.

KING LIR: Lock them in their cabins!

ARYEL: *(imitating Edmon's voice)* Lock me up! What right have you to lock me up? We're giving the orders around here now! We're republicans! Up the Republic of Ecstasy!

KING LIR: This is treason! Arrest them. Get the guillotine ready!

SAILOR: What the hell's that?

KING LIR: Just catch them, you idiot!

ARYEL: *(going behind Kaspalto, and imitating Yago's voice)* Up the Republic of Ecstasy-Lovers!

KASPALTO: *(singing)* Donn mwa de boutey Bay Kedou
Samdji mo pey twa. *(he starts to dance.)*
Ecstasy-lovers! Diwana, mastana! Ecstasy-lovers!

(The sailor and Poloniouss move in on Kaspalto and Dammarro. Aryel slaps them. The two lads believe that they pulled off this amazing feat. The king runs to hide.)

DAMMARRO: Did you see that, Yago? I just blow, and they all fall down like ripe fruit from the tree!

KASPALTO: Mari[10], man!

ARYEL: *(picks them up and carries them off.)* Up the Republic of Hedonism! No more Kings! Long live Edmon, President of the Republic! Long live Yago, Prime Minister!

POLONIOUSS: *(emerging from hiding)* Oh my God! They can fly.....

---

9   "Basen" is the word for "pond" or "lake" in Mauritian Creole. Grand Basen is the island's Hindu holy lake. We've left the word untranslated here for obvious reasons.
10   "Mari" translates (roughly) as "Crazy!": but it's a very idiomatic Mauritian expression, and doesn't really need translating here.

ACT 2. Scene 2.

(In Prospero's control room. Prospero and Kalibann.)

KALIBANN:	Nothing too complicated - just a loose jack. That's why the screen was playing up.
PROSPERO:	You learn fast, Kalibann. Don't think I haven't noticed. Nowadays you do all the maintenance and repair work. You've even made a few improvements. I want you to know that, even though I may at times appear a little hard on you, I do appreciate the work you do. When all this is over, I intend to give you your freedom. *(Pause.)* Well - come on then - tell me how pleased you are.
KALIBANN:	Mr. Prospero, if we don't take care, there are going to be problems with the central computer.
PROSPERO:	What do you mean?
KALIBANN:	We're overloading on the central brain. Any chip failure would mean the whole system crashing.
PROSPERO:	Don't worry - nothing'll go wrong. It's a foolproof system.
KALIBANN:	Of course, sir. But, if I could make one suggestion, if we made a series of interdependent brains, then if one did break down, another could take over.
PROSPERO:	There's no need. It's better to have one central intelligence which controls everything. The central brain gives me absolute power.... Just a minute - let me finish. The central brain is indestructible. I'm completely sure of that. *(Pause.)* I asked you a question, and you haven't answered. Are you glad that I'm giving you your freedom?
KALIBANN:	Freedom?
PROSPERO:	Yes, freedom.
KALIBANN:	But I am already free, Mr. Prospero.
PROSPERO:	Well, I suppose you're free to do what I tell you.
KALIBANN:	You've never stood in my way.
PROSPERO:	Perhaps you've always wanted to do as I wished.
KALIBANN:	No problem, then.
PROSPERO:	But what happens if some day you want to do something which I don't agree to? Hunh?
KALIBANN:	Then I suppose you would have to remind me of my mother's promise.
PROSPERO:	Exactly! And that's what I mean by freedom. The cancellation of that promise.

KALIBANN: Thank you.

PROSPERO: You don't exactly seem overcome with emotion.

KALIBANN: How would you and Miss Kordelia manage without me? I've been looking after your work for so long -

PROSPERO: Don't worry about it. I have other plans for Kordelia and myself. That's up to me. It's good of you to think about us, but you needn't. I know what I'm doing.

KALIBANN: You must be very strong, Mr. Prospero. You seem not to need anybody else; but everybody - Kordelia, Aryel, myself, the people from the ship - we all need you.

PROSPERO: That's the power of science.

KALIBANN: What will you do with them?

PROSPERO: Who?

KALIBANN: The people from the ship.

PROSPERO: I'll nibble pistachios and watch the movie.

KALIBANN: It's a pretty sad film.

PROSPERO: I don't know what's happening to everybody today! Feelings confusing your brains! Go and set up the second projection. Check the slides, the reels, the audio and the video. *(Enter Aryel.)* OK, Aryel?

ARYEL: Haven't you been watching?

PROSPERO: Of course. Perfect work.

ARYEL: I've put the two clowns in prison, and I've released Yago and Edmon to return to the ship. There they are on the screen! (Pause) Captain, can I go and see Prince Ferdjinan now? Like we said?

PROSPERO: Is this absolutely necessary?

ARYEL: If I make myself visible to him, it will help the trickery.

KALIBANN: *(to Aryel)* There's bound to be trouble if you get too close to him.

ARYEL: *(to Kalibann)* Mind your own business. Or I'll spill the beans about you two.

PROSPERO: What are you saying?

ARYEL: I was just telling him to change the way Prince Ferdjinan's prison is decorated. He should be made to feel more at home.

PROSPERO: Do you really think so?

ARYEL: Don't you trust me, Captain?

PROSPERO: Well, of course, but -

ARYEL: Whatever you say.

PROSPERO: Fine! All right! Go ahead.

(Aryel and Kalibann go out.)

ACT 2. Scene 3.

(On board the ship. King Lir and Poloniouss.)

POLONIOUSS: This place ought to be a Paradise. I look out and I see water all around us - a fertile, luxuriant natural beauty. Everything humanity could ask for. So why does this Paradise have the stench of Hell? The tension's growing by the minute. Everyone's so irritated.... As if the Paradise were a giant illusion, a great lie, and the reality is that we're sitting on a volcano[11] that's about to blow. Lir, I can't soothe your pain any more. My own pain is casting a shadow across my mind.

KING LIR: Your pain?

POLONIOUSS: It takes time to change a way of thinking. I thought that this experience we are going through might force people to look at themselves, and search for a new way to live. I was wrong.

KING LIR: Explain.

POLONIOUSS: I'm thinking of Yago and Edmon. This experience has simply brought out the beast in them. They've no discipline, no sense of responsibility to the community - they just fly away.

(The sailor enters, in a hurry.)

SAILOR: Majesty, they're coming back.

KING LIR: Who do you mean?

SOLDIER: THEM!

POLONIOUSS: Let me deal with him - he's frightened. Don't panic, son. Breathe deeply. Stay calm. You should make it a rule of life never to panic. Understood? Now tell His Majesty what you saw.

SAILOR: Edmon and Yago!

POLONIOUSS: Oh my God! Run for your lives! Run, everybody!

(Poloniouss hides. Edmon and Yago enter.)

KING LIR: No fighting. No killing. You can take it all. Ship, throne, kingdom. Up the Republic of Ecstasy. Hail to the President.

EDMON: Lir, what's up with you? This is weird, Yago! He's gone mad with grief.

---

11   Mauritius is, of course, a volcanic island. There is a dormant volcano at its centre, Trou aux Cerfs. The neighbouring island of La Reunion has an active volcano.

KING LIR:	Yes, I'm mad. I abdicate! Take all my power. Put me on a raft - let me go and make a new life somewhere on the far side of the ocean.
YAGO:	Did you say "abdicate", your majesty?
KING LIR:	Yes, I have abdicated. Power tends to corrupt and absolute power corrupts absolutely. I therefore command that power be given to the people. Organise an election.
EDMON:	We've got to knock some sense into him, Yago.
KING LIR:	Don't you knock me! I'm already knocked out. And I've done far too much knocking in my time. No more knocking - please, no more!
YAGO:	Take him to his cabin! He shouldn't be seen in this state.

(The sailor takes out the King.)

YAGO:	Your Majesty, King Edmon.
EDMON:	Are you quite well?
YAGO:	Your brother has abdicated. Prince Ferdjinan has disappeared. You're next in line to the throne. Power, it would seem, has fallen into our hands without any effort at all.
EDMON:	Our hands?
YAGO:	I mean - your hands.
EDMON:	So what should I do?
YAGO:	Call a meeting. Get him to abdicate formally in a public situation. Make him hand over power to you in front of witnesses. We need to look for Poloniouss.
POLONIOUSS:	*(from hiding)* Don't hit me. I'll do whatever you ask. Remember my age.
YAGO:	Did you hear that? A demon on the ship?
POLONIOUSS:	*(coming out)* No, it wasn't a demon, it was me. I'm your witness. King Lir has abdicated... I witnessed it...
EDMON:	Why are you shaking like that?
YAGO:	Perhaps he's got Parkinson's.
EDMON:	My kingdom is diseased.
YAGO:	It doesn't matter if the country is nothing but a combined prison, hospital, asylum and cemetery. Power is all that counts! Call a meeting! Poloniouss, you may be the

main performer on this historic occasion. Your chance to make a particularly memorable speech. One which students of history and politics will make the subject of tomes in years to come.

POLONIOUSS: What do I have to say?

YAGO: You're the expert speech-maker. Do you really need help from me? Well.... Something about rights, duties and responsibilities. Something about impotence, incompetence, incompatibility. Something about the abdication, the handover of power, the coronation. A new dawn, a new tomorrow, a new future for the nation. Et cetera.[12]

---

12   In the London production, the Interval was at this point. We preserved Virahsawmy's three act structure by using projected titles for the Phases of Prospero's plan.

ACT 2. Scene 4.

(Ferdjinan and Aryel)

FERDJINAN:	It was a dark, humid, filthy prison I was in. Then suddenly - ker-pow! It turns into a five-star suite with plush furniture and air-con.... Ever since this morning, it's just been one miracle after another. If they are miracles. Dreams? Oh, I don't know. Maybe mirages, shimmering in the desert.
ARYEL:	On our island, these are everyday events. They are trivial here.
FERDJINAN:	Who are you?
ARYEL:	We have met before.
FERDJINAN:	I don't remember.
ARYEL:	Still.... Another miracle.
FERDJINAN:	How long have I got to live with miracles?
ARYEL:	According to Aristotle, 24 hours is the limit. According to Prospero - 12.
FERDJINAN:	So it's a game?
ARYEL:	You could say that. A complicated game which began twenty years ago. In every game, there are tough moments, and this is one of them. I think you need to become a player yourself.
FERDJINAN:	I thought I already was.
ARYEL:	You're in the game, but only as a pawn. If you take hold of the pieces, you can move things on.
FERDJINAN:	All right. Tell me what I need to do.
ARYEL:	I have my plans for you.
FERDJINAN:	Oh what a pleasant change.
ARYEL:	Why do you say that?
FERDJINAN:	From the moment I was born, people have had their plans for me. As if I was a puppet or something. My father has his plan: I'm supposed to make a politically advantageous match with some princess or other, and prepare to mount his throne.... I thought maybe after the shipwreck I'd be freed in some way; but that was just hot air. Where do I fit in? Can't I make my own plans and live my own life?
ARYEL:	I'm sorry. I hadn't thought of it that way. My guru, Prospero, has never spoken of this. The way things happen here, he and I make the plans for everybody else. It's considered normal. Plans are made by the knowledgeable and the strong. The

others just have to go along with it.

FERDJINAN: You sound like Yago.

ARYEL: No -

FERDJINAN: Yes. He's always making plans for people.

ARYEL: The difference is that our plans are to secure a better future for everybody.

FERDJINAN: And do you ask the people if they agree?

ARYEL: That isn't necessary.

FERDJINAN: It's fundamental! It's a big mistake to think that what we want for other people is what they want for themselves.

ARYEL: How can you know?

FERDJINAN: Ask them.

ARYEL: OK - what do you want for yourself?

FERDJINAN: That's the one thing I'm not at all sure of.

ARYEL: See?

FERDJINAN: But I'm sure of what I don't want: I don't want to marry and I don't want to be king.

ARYEL: But you'll ruin everything.

FERDJINAN: So would you take my place?

ARYEL: Hey?

FERDJINAN: Get married to Kordelia. Be king. Live happily ever after.

ARYEL: It's not in my programme!

FERDJINAN: What?

ARYEL: Oh no - I've gone and said more than I should. Captain will be furious.

FERDJINAN: Who's Captain?

ARYEL: Prospero. My inventor.

FERDJINAN: Do you mean your father?

ARYEL: No.

FERDJINAN: Stop pulling my leg.

ARYEL: It's true.

FERDJINAN: You're a robot?

ARYEL: Yes and no. A robot, but almost a human. The only difference is that I'm not capable of reproduction. I'm without sex.

FERDJINAN: Oh. Well... do you have desires? And... feelings, and... things?

ARYEL: I think so.

FERDJINAN: Tell me what you're thinking now. What you're feeling.

ARYEL: I'm thinking - I'm thinking how you and I could work together. How we could make a life together. How we could help Prospero and Kordelia. I'm feeling - I'm feeling that I like you very much. And I feel very sorry for your father.

FERDJINAN: Why?

ARYEL: Edmon and Yago have forced him to abdicate. Edmon has made himself king.

FERDJINAN: Have they hurt him?

ARYEL: No. But he has lost his power.

FERDJINAN: I am free!

ARYEL: Aren't you scared of Edmon and Yago?

FERDJINAN: No. Just let them go. Then you and I, my father, Prospero, Kordelia and Kalibann can live here in peace.

ARYEL: That's not possible.

FERDJINAN: Why?

ARYEL: Because this island is phase to be passed through. We all have to emerge from it, and return to reality.

FERDJINAN: Isn't this reality? You and me - aren't we real?

ARYEL: Imagine that we are in our mother's womb. When the time comes, we have to leave. You can't fight it - there's a force which is pushing us out. This island is a zone which people pass through in order to become different -

FERDJINAN: Which makes us twin brothers!

ARYEL: I suppose so.

FERDJINAN:	Fantastic!
ARYEL:	Why the excitement?
FERDJINAN:	Because it's so extraordinary. We're two children formed in the same womb. We're different but at the same time (he throws his arms round Aryel's neck.) What's the matter?
ARYEL:	I'm not programmed to express my feelings. Physical contact disrupts the balance of my chips. If you continue to touch me, I shall lose control.
FERDJINAN:	Then lose control! You need to. Why is everybody so serious? Why not play, jump, spring, turn cartwheels like a child? Forget about convention! You and I can live happily together, wherever we are!
ARYEL:	Do you know what you're saying?
FERDJINAN:	Yes! Aryel, yes. Forget about convention.

(A big noise.)

ARYEL:	Oh no - I'd forgotten about them.
FERDJINAN:	Who?
ARYEL:	Wait, I'll be right back.

(he goes out.)

| FERDJINAN: | What's happening to me? I'm supposed to be a Prince -the heir to the throne. Suddenly, here I am deciding to throw it all away and live a simple life like ordinary people. I just want to forget the responsibilities other people have lumbered me with. I want to spend my life with a person who isn't even human - with a machine who isn't really a machine... The island's magical all right. Like a whirlwind over the sea, it lifts the still waters which were dormant at the bottom, until they're waves tossing on the surface. |

(Aryel comes back with Kaspalto and Dammarro.)

	What are those two doing here?
KASPALTO:	Your Highness! Dammarro - pinch me, man! I wanna know if I's dreamin'!
DAMMARRO:	Man - I've been dreaming all day. Prince Ferdjinan, isn't it?
FERDJINAN:	I was Prince Ferdjinan. But I have decided to give up my title, and the privileges which go with it.
KASPALTO:	No way!
ARYEL:	I don't think Mr. Prospero will agree to that. His plan -

FERDJINAN: Let me talk to him.

ARYEL: Good luck. Listen, all of you - there's something we've got to do. King Lir's in trouble. Edmon and Yago have deposed him. Edmon's made himself King and Yago Prime Minister. We've got to put things back in order.

FERDJINAN: What kind of order?

ARYEL: Put your father back on the throne.

FERDJINAN: But everything would just stay the same. Why not look for another king? Why not abolish the monarchy altogether?

ARYEL: Calm down! The priority is to deal with Edmon and Yago. We can worry about constitutional issues afterwards.

KASPALTO: *(to Aryel)* Hey, man! I know you! I dunno your face, but I sure as hell remembers your voice.

ARYEL: You drink too much, and see what happens.... Now, help me think.

ACT 2. Scene 5.

(On the ship. In King Lir's cabin.)

KING LIR: You see, Poloniouss, it is on earth that our sins are expiated. We think that because we are strong or powerful, we can do as we please - but look what is happening to us now. We went along with Edmon and Yago in deposing Prospero. Poor man: heaven knows where he is now. Look what is happening to us. All day I've been thinking of Prospero and his child. Think - today she could have been a young woman. Beautiful like her mother. The perfect woman for my son. I've lost it all. My son, my kingdom, everything. But do you know what scares me most of all? I feel that I have lost my soul.

POLONIOUSS: Your majesty...

KING LIR: Don't call me that.

POLONIOUSS: To me, you will always be a king; even though you have lost your crown.

KING LIR: Oh Poloniouss - I need to ask for your forgiveness too. I turned on you: I was angry - I didn't want to admit my own mistakes. So often you've tried to stop me going wrong. You saw when I was going off the rails, but whenever you tried to show me the error of my ways, I'd just get angry with you. Now, I find myself wishing that you hadn't let me intimidate you.

POLONIOUSS: Your Majesty - I have my own confession to make.

KING LIR: Don't be afraid to tell me.

POLONIOUSS: That day we set Prospero and Kordelia adrift on the raft, I disobeyed you.

KING LIR: What did you do?

POLONIOUSS: I secretly gave Prospero some food and clothes. And his favourite books.

KING LIR: You did?

POLONIOUSS: Please don't be angry. It felt like the right thing to do...

KING LIR: I'm not in the slightest bit angry. God, if only - It's better not to think about it.

POLONIOUSS: Don't give up hope. Where there's a will, there's a way.

KING LIR: My dear Poloniouss. Now I really appreciate you. You accept all my caprice - have done for years. I'm a monster, Poloniouss.

POLONIOUSS: No, Majesty. You're a human being; and, like all human beings, you make mistakes. The sign of a good man is that he recognises the mistakes he's made.

(Sailor knocks on the door, and enters.)

SAILOR:	Majesty!
POLONIOUSS:	You see! In the eyes of the people, you are still the King!
KING LIR:	Yes, my son, what is it?
SAILOR:	Prince Edmon -
POLONIOUSS:	King.
SAILOR:	Yes, sir. He says he needs you.
KING LIR:	He needs me?!
POLONIOUSS:	Majesty - they're writing the script now. Best to play your part in the comedy.
KING LIR:	Yes. Yes, you're right. Where is he?
SAILOR:	In the throne room. Your former royal apartment.
POLONIOUSS:	Power's new to him, and he wants to enjoy it to the full. Where on earth will it end?
KING LIR:	Time, Poloniouss. Let Time do the work.

ACT 2. Scene 6.

(On the ship - the new throne room. Edmon and Yago.)

EDMON: Prime Minister Yago, to inaugurate my reign, we need to establish a policy of universal order.

YAGO: Certainly, Your Majesty. However, in order to permit a policy of universal order, there must first be universal chaos. The question therefore arises: how do we begin to create chaos?

EDMON: Perhaps with a policy of fun. There is a general excess of seriousness amongst my subjects. A lack of frivolity. I don't even have a court jester. Imagine - what sort of a monarchy is this? I want a jester. And dancing - I want all the sailors to dance. A policy of universal mirth. My eternal reign should go down in history as the Golden Age of clowning.

SAILOR: Will that be all, Your Majesty?

EDMON: No. Where's Lir? I sent for him, didn't I?

SAILOR: I've summoned him, sir.

YAGO: Look, he's here.

(Enter King Lir and Poloniouss.)

EDMON: Kneel before your king!

POLONIOUSS: Your Majesty. Your power is absolute....Your wish is our command. But think of your brother, your unfortunate elder brother. Better not to show disrespect....

EDMON: Not show disrespect? Never. I permit you to stand.

KING LIR: I'll stay kneeling. It's good for my varicose veins.

EDMON: There Poloniouss! I know what's best for him! Splendid. Now - there is a serious issue to discuss. We need to get in touch with that really wealthy king - the one whose daughter was engaged to Ferdjinan - and tell him that I have taken his place.

KING LIR: How are we to do that?

EDMON: That's your problem. My wish is your command, and at the moment I wish to consolidate my power and prosperity through this inter-dynastic marriage. In the event that I do not receive a favourable reply to my suit, one head will be chopped off. I trust that this is understood. Poloniouss, you're good with words. I give you the task of preparing an historic oration to be delivered on the occasion of my marriage. And I don't want any repetition of what happened at the coronation. Fancy making a mockery of such a glorious event by telling the story of the hare and the tortoise.

POLONIOUSS:	I was using metaphor, Your Majesty.
EDMON:	I don't care what you were using metal for - I want a better speech at the Royal Wedding! Now, Yago - back to the policy of dancing. I should like an erotic dance to grace my royal presence. Belly-dancing, strip-tease - that sort of thing. This is what is required for the well-being of the kingdom.

(Erotic music plays. A female dancer appears and gyrates sexily. When the dance is over...)[13]

YAGO:	Your Majesty? Where are you? Oh no... The king's been kidnapped! Edmon, Edmon, where are you?
EDMON:	*(from behind the throne)* Wait!
YAGO:	What are you doing round there?
EDMON:	Aaaaah! Now - that's what I call royal power! Eh, Yago! I'm amazing! I just have to wish for something, and it happens. I'm even better than a King, I'm like -
VOICE:	*(The voice of Prospero, but it's not clear where it's coming from, and now only Edmon can hear it.)* God.
EDMON:	That's right!.... Who said that? Was it you, Yago.
YAGO:	Not me.
EDMON:	Poloniouss?
POLONIOUSS:	No, Your Majesty.
VOICE:	It's me.
EDMON:	Lir?
KING LIR:	No.
VOICE:	It's me.
EDMON:	*(looking at the ceiling)* Who are you?
VOICE:	I am yourself. You are myself. I am your mind, and everything that you desire.
EDMON:	Did you hear that, Yago? Hot stuff! Everything I desire? Everything?
VOICE:	Yes.
EDMON:	I desire a huge banquet, with the best booze and really beautiful women - I want it before my very eyes.

---

13   Although it's not explicit in the text, this is clearly a reference to the sega: a Mauritian folk dance which involves the female dancers lifting their skirts and gyrating their hips. Once frowned upon as lewd, the dance has acquired a new popularity through performance in tourist hotels.

VOICE:	Before your very eyes?
EDMON:	That's what I said.

(Magical music. A banquet is brought in. The table is laden with food, champagne, wine etc. Waiters and waitresses rush around busily.)

EDMON:	I ask you all to join me in raising your glasses to drink the health of the new king. What's this? They're all paralysed. (He tries to raise his glass, but cannot.) You wicked voice - you've betrayed me!
VOICE:	Oh no, Your Majesty. You said that you wanted a banquet before your very eyes. That's what you got. What more do you want?
EDMON:	I want more!
VOICE:	No.
EDMON:	I want to eat.
VOICE:	No.
EDMON:	Why?!
VOICE:	It's not a part of the bargain.
EDMON:	What bargain?
VOICE:	There are certain conditions.
EDMON:	Change them!
VOICE:	That cannot be done.
EDMON:	Why not?
VOICE:	Because I say so.
EDMON:	Who the hell are you?
VOICE:	I am yourself. You are myself.
EDMON:	You're out of your mind?
VOICE:	You're out of your mind.
EDMON:	Are you calling me mad?
VOICE:	I am mad, you are mad.
EDMON:	Stop him! Put him in prison! Hang him! Yago - arrest him.

VOICE:	Yago - arrest him.
EDMON:	Didn't you hear me? Put him in prison!
VOICE:	Didn't you hear me? Put him in prison.
EDMON:	I give the orders!
VOICE:	I give the orders.
EDMON:	*(in panic)* It's a demon! Sod off, demon! Aaah!

(He rushes out.)

KING LIR:	What's got in to him?
YAGO:	Don't ask me - he's your brother. How should I know? I'm only a Prime Minister.
POLONIOUSS:	Are you hedging your bets again?
YAGO:	I've just about had enough of this. Every time something goes wrong, they all look for me. Need somebody to blame? Oh yes - let's all blame Yago. Ever since that little runt Shakespeare used me to stir things up between Othello and his wife, everyone thinks I'm to blame for everything that goes wrong anywhere in the whole world!
POLONIOUSS:	You deposed Prospero, didn't you? Even though he'd given you so much... your own brother! And you deposed King Lir! Edmon's behaving like a lunatic, so you're hedging your bets again! And now, to cap it all, you decide you want to be canonised!
YAGO:	Now hang on a minute! Who was it offered me Prospero's throne in return for an alliance? Hunh?
KING LIR:	Oh don't rake all that up again! What about the way you deposed me? Hunh?
YAGO:	It was hardly a case of deposing you! We saw you shaking like a leaf. Poloniouss was in hiding. We had to take command for the good of the state!
POLONIOUSS:	Well, that's your way of looking at it. It's all a question of viewpoint.
YAGO:	Whatever your viewpoint, this whole thing is turning into a farce. Can't you see that it's all somebody's play? There's no logic to it otherwise.... OK - I'll go and find the dunce. Just in case he starts to take his role too seriously.

(As he starts to go, Edmon appears. He is dressed and armed like Rambo.)

EDMON:	Where is he? I'll fill him with holes. A sieve-demon!
VOICE:	Is it me you're looking for, Edmon?

EDMON: Where are you?

(He shoots the machine gun everywhere.)

KING LIR: Stop him, you idiots - there'll be a disaster!

POLONIOUSS: How are we supposed to do that? The men have all run away... Edmon.... Forgive me, Your Majesty, but please would you give me your toy?

EDMON: Where is he? Search!

POLONIOUSS: Give me the machine gun. I'll find him for you.

(Machine gun noises. Edmon rushes out, followed by Lir, Poloniouss and Sailor)

YAGO: Oh this is ridiculous! Everybody wants to be King, and look what happens. Come back Prospero! It's your time now!

VOICE: Yago - you are calling me. Do you need me now?

YAGO: I need you. Yes, I need you.[14]

---

14   This is the section of the play where we have taken ther greatest liberty in departing from the original text. In the original, Edmon is shown his reflection in a mirror, and goes mad.

ACT 2. Scene 7.

(In Prospero's control room. Kordelia and Kalibann.)

KALIBANN:	You're joking?
KORDELIA:	I swear!
KALIBANN:	So - why tell me?
KORDELIA:	In case you got jealous.
KALIBANN:	What have I got to be jealous about?
KORDELIA:	I thought... just a bit. A little pinch at the heart. No?
KALIBANN:	*(smiling)* So what are you going to do?
KORDELIA:	There's nothing I can do. Ferdjinan doesn't have the same taste as you, anyway. I get the feeling he's more interested in Aryel.
KALIBANN:	Really? You know Aryel fancies him as well? What a lovely couple. Shocking.
KORDELIA:	I sometimes think it's impossible to shock me. It's because all I know is what I've lived on this island, or read in Dad's books. When the whole world is extraordinary, nothing is shocking. All I've ever really known about love is Dad and his machines, you and me, and now Ferdjinan and Aryel. How much knowledge is that? I think I know that the human race is very beautiful; but that there are ugly creatures among the beauty. No, that's too harsh, isn't it? What I should say is that there is good and bad in all of us, but that sometimes the bad comes out on top.
KALIBANN:	I find it all very confusing myself. In one book I read that people are born bad, and society - that's a word I didn't really understand - needs to control them. Then another book said that people are born good and this thing called society spoils them. I don't know. I haven't met enough people to generalise about them. I know you, I know your father - I suppose I know myself a bit... and apart from that I've just seen a few blobs moving around the video monitors.
KORDELIA:	And now there's Ferdjinan. And I know a bit of history - what those men did to my mother twenty years ago. I think I've got some understanding of the comic ways of those blobs on the monitors. They all seem a bit mad to me. Except Poloniouss, perhaps. But even he's a bit... Well, he's a good man, but a bit ineffectual. Like a yogi.
KALIBANN:	More like a yoyo.
KORDELIA:	Maybe they're the same thing..... Am I stopping you working?
KALIBANN:	No - but if you helped me it would get done quicker. Your father will be back any minute. He's told me to get things ready for Phase Three.

KORDELIA:	And what happens then?
KALIBANN:	I'm afraid it's all going to bounce back on him. There are things he hasn't bargained for.
KORDELIA:	Like what?
KALIBANN:	Ferdjinan's inclinations, for one thing.
KORDELIA:	Anything else?
KALIBANN:	Oh, come on, Kordi, use your pretty head.
KORDELIA:	That is so patronising! Just because you've read more-
KALIBANN:	So what have you been reading? Simone de Beauvoir?
KORDELIA:	I can think for myself.
KALIBANN:	You certainly can. You've got the perfect recipe for brain chutney.
KORDELIA:	Just like my father! You've got to be so bloody macho, haven't you?
KALIBANN:	Bravo, Kordi! Come here you!

(He grabs and kisses her.)

KORDELIA:	Get off! Cool it! Dad's coming.
KALIBANN:	He's not coming yet. What are you scared of?
KORDELIA:	You prepare his Phase Three. Ours comes later. Oh, Kal... didn't he say anything to you?
KALIBANN:	Nothing important. Oh, hang on - there was something, but I didn't really understand it. He said he was going to give me my freedom. Do you know what all that's about?
KORDELIA:	You are such a buffoon, Mr. Kalibann. An electronics expert who doesn't understand the most basic things. Once you've got your freedom, he can't make you do anything. Do you understand?
KALIBANN:	No.
KORDELIA:	Listen, Kal. If he comes now, and tells you to do something, do you have to do it? Yes or no?
KALIBANN:	Yes.
KORDELIA:	Well, being free means you can say no.

KALIBANN: But how would he cope if I said no? He depends on me.

KORDELIA: That's not what he thinks. He thinks he doesn't depend on anything or anybody - he's free, independent, autonomous. That's why he can be so authoritarian.

KALIBANN: Where did you learn to criticise him? He's taught us all we know.

KORDELIA: Call it female intuition.

KALIBANN: What's that?

KORDELIA: Something which macho men don't understand.

(Enter Prospero)

PROSPERO: Everything set, Kalibann?

KALIBANN: Yes, sir.

PROSPERO: Good. *(He sees Kordelia)* What are you doing here? Aren't you supposed to be getting to know Prince Ferdjinan?

KORDELIA: I've already got to know your adored future son-in-law.

PROSPERO: And you're happy with him?

KORDELIA: Perfectly.

PROSPERO: Very good. Everything's going to plan. Kalibann, countdown for Phase Three. Ten. Nine. Eight. Seven.....

*

ACT 3. Scene 1.

(Storm: thunder, lightning, hail, rain. Poloniouss and the Sailor.)

SAILOR: You again! Come on, grand-dad, do us all a service. Get back to your cabin.

POLONIOUSS: Still in a bad mood, eh'?

SAILOR: You're not safe on deck. See? Back to your cabin.

POLONIOUSS: How's anything going to happen to our ship? We're on a pond. We're hardly going to drown, are we?

SAILOR: You think so? We could capsize any minute!

POLONIOUSS: Then it's better to stay on deck, isn't it!

SAILOR: Oh, do as you please, then.[15] But don't forget we were only saved by a miracle last time. The King keeps saying that you pay for your sins on earth. If I wasn't a loyal subject I'd be saying my prayers now.

POLONIOUSS: Nature is in a rage and whipping our consciences. Prospero... Prospero!

VOICE: Yes, Poloniouss.

POLONIOUSS: I'd sensed your presence already.

VOICE: I am everywhere, Poloniouss.

SAILOR: Is it a ghost?

POLONIOUSS: Prospero, you've proved your strength; you've won the battle. What more do you want?

VOICE: My thirst for revenge has been satisfied. Everything will be made clear tonight.

(The storm calms down. The mountains disappear. The ship stands on the sand in the middle of a desert. The desert is surrounded by the sea.)

SAILOR: Now we're stranded in a desert! Oh God, this is hopeless!

POLONIOUSS: Sand everywhere. A burning sun.

(The sailor is searching helplessly for water.)

POLONIOUSS: Prospero - why have you done this to us. Prospero! Prospero, why don't you say anything?.... He has abandoned us.

(Ferdjinan enters, with Aryel, Kaspalto and Dammarro.)

---

15   This is the one scene which suffers from our reduction in the number of sailors. In the original Creole text, two sailors have quite a lengthy scene here, which we've compressed.

	Ferdjinan? Is that you? Are you in this Hell too?
FERDJINAN:	Hell? What do you mean, Hell?
POLONIOUSS:	Oh no - the heat must have turned his brain. Come into the shade....
FERDJINAN:	Uncle Poloniouss - what's happening to you? You seem so very old.
POLONIOUSS:	I feel as if I've lived through an eternity in the course of one day. Where have you been? Your father thinks you're dead. Well, perhaps we all are. Perhaps we're meeting in Hell to pay for our sins.
FERDJINAN:	No, Uncle Poloniouss. We're alive. Very much alive. This is a magic island.... If you knew everything I've seen, you'd probably have a heart attack.
POLONIOUSS:	I'd better call your father. Oh, my mind's gone blank. I don't understand anything any more.

(He goes.)

FERDJINAN:	(to Sailor.) Oi, you! Don't loaf about. Bring all the equipment and tools, and get the whole crew - I said the whole crew - here at the double.

(The sailor goes.)

ARYEL:	What are you up to?
FERDJINAN:	If you want to stop people from panicking, you get them to do something. We're going to dig a canal from the ship to the ocean. Kaspalto!
KASPALTO:	Yes, boss.
FERDJINAN:	I'm putting you and Dammarro in charge of restoration.
DAMMARRO:	Restor- what?
FERDJINAN:	You know - ammunition.
DAMMARRO:	Ah, you mean...
FERDJINAN:	Yes, I do. You know where to find the stock-pile, I presume.
DAMMARRO:	No problem boss.

(Kaspalto and Dammarro go about their business.)

ARYEL:	They'll only get legless.
FERDJINAN:	I don't think so. Everybody needs a little bit of "oomph" from time to time: it helps them forget their troubles. The best way to get people to work is to wipe out their

memories. We all need some sort of dream to keep our lives going. But they understand as well as we do that nothing comes easily. You've got to sweat for it.

(Poloniouss and King Lir come in.)

KING LIR: Ferdjinan.... is it really you? Or another mirage?

FERDJINAN: No, father - it's me.

KING LIR: A miracle. My son is alive.... Who is this?

FERDJINAN: This is Aryel. He lives on the island.

KING LIR: You mean to say the island is inhabited?

FERDJINAN: It certainly is! You'll be surprised who lives here.

POLONIOUSS: Prospero.

FERDJINAN: In the flesh.

KING LIR: So he survived? What about the little girl?

ARYEL: They're both living here.

KING LIR: How did they manage to save themselves?

ARYEL: They had food, clothes and books. You gave them a bit of secret help there, didn't you, Poloniouss? Prospero's been waiting on this island - preparing to return with his new knowledge and power.

POLONIOUSS: He means to return then?

ARYEL: Oh yes. Everything that has happened to you here has been his doing. He knows everything we're saying. All over the island there are cameras and microphones. Nothing can happen without his say-so.

KING LIR: So why has he sent you instead of coming to talk to us himself?

ARYEL: He didn't send me: I came with Ferdjinan. Captain - I call him Captain - Prospero will never forgive me for that.

POLONIOUSS: Tell me about his daughter... What was her name? Mir... no - Kordelia.

FERDJINAN: A beautiful young woman. A royal beauty.

KING LIR: Well, in that case....

FERDJINAN: No you don't! Aren't you fed up with making plans for other people's lives?

KING LIR: What?

FERDJINAN:	You're so obsessed with getting married and breeding. All this nonsense about inheritance.
KING LIR:	But our inheritance is who we are!
FERDJINAN:	No! We are.... Oh - you'll never understand. Let's find a way out of here. Aryel, have you any idea how we might dig this canal?
ARYEL:	But Captain -
FERDJINAN:	Will you forget about Prospero for a minute? We're free. The only reason that he seems strong is that we've been weak. We've been waiting to be saved. Well, nobody is going to save us. We've got the intelligence, the courage and the will.
KASPALTO:	What a speech, man!
DAMMARRO:	Wild.
FERDJINAN:	You're paralysed because of what your conscience is doing to your soul. You're finding it impossible to act because the mistakes of the past are getting in the way of today's reasoning. But you have to understand that things have changed.
ARYEL:	Ferdjinan -
FERDJINAN:	Aryel, you're the one who made me see clearly. Prospero may have made you, but he hasn't been able to stop you having feelings. He can threaten you as much as he wants: today you are free. You're free because you have dared. We have to dare.

(Yago comes in.)

YAGO:	Would somebody please help me get this man out from under his bed? Ever since Toufann -
FERDJINAN:	You called it Toufann?
YAGO:	Oh - you've come back. (Pause) Well, Toufann is the name of the cyclone, isn't it?
FERDJINAN:	Yes. But how do you know?
YAGO:	I'm not sure. It just slipped out.
FERDJINAN:	You see! Now Prospero can even make you think the way he wants. Don't let him! You'll end up as his puppets, like Kalibann.
POLONIOUSS:	Kanibel?
FERDJINAN:	Another inhabitant. The owner of the island before Prospero came.
POLONIOUSS:	And are there many of these cannibals?

ARYEL:	Kalibann is the name of a person. His father was a white pirate, and his mother a black slave. He's a mulatto.
POLONIOUSS:	Oh no - how awful for him!
ARYEL:	You don't have to feel sorry for him. He knows what he wants.
YAGO:	This is all well and good; but His Majesty is currently hiding under his bed, and I'd like some-one's help to get him out.
FERDJINAN:	Aryel, you go. Bring him here and give him a spade. He can help dig the canal.

(Aryel and Yago go.)

KING LIR:	Ferdjinan... there's something I have to tell you. I didn't tell you the whole truth about Prospero. I have been to blame...
FERDJINAN:	I know. But that doesn't give him the right to play with people's lives. He has no right to play at God, using his power for revenge. If only he could learn a bit of compassion, that might change it all.
POLONIOUSS:	Ferdjinan - you've grown into rather a fine young man. I think your reign...
FERDJINAN:	What reign?
POLONIOUSS:	Well, you have to succeed your father.
KING LIR:	Of course. The country needs you.
FERDJINAN:	We'll see about that.

(Aryel and Yago carry on Edmon.)

YAGO:	His Majesty King Edmon the First.
EDMON:	Ah! It's horrible! Look - a ghost! Ferdjinan! Not me - him! Yago did it! He made me do it! Don't hurt me....
FERDJINAN:	Uncle Edmon!
EDMON:	No! No! No! (faints)
FERDJINAN:	The monarchy appears to be in crisis.

(The Sailor enters, running.)

SAILOR:	Who's giving the orders now? There's a tidal wave heading straight towards us!
FERDJINAN:	Take your orders from me.
SAILOR:	The radar shows a wave as high as a mountain. The island will be completely

flooded. What can we do?

ARYEL: Don't do anything. It's just an illusion. A virtual reality projection.

VOICE: Aryel! You traitor! Just wait - I'm coming myself!

(Prospero appears. Panic from everyone except Ferdjinan and Aryel.)

PROSPERO: Ah-ha! Frightening, hunh? You're all frozen with terror!

FERDJINAN: Yes, Prospero. Everybody's paralysed with fear. Everybody's terrified of you. Does it make you happy?

PROSPERO: You wait - you get to speak in a moment. Poloniouss, only you deserve my forgiveness. In my moment of deepest despair, you were the one who helped me. But you, Lir...

KING LIR: I know, I know. Do whatever you want - I deserve it. I've already abdicated. Tell me what else you want of me.

PROSPERO: I want your son to marry my daughter.

KING LIR: I agree.

PROSPERO: And then he should become King instead of you.

KING LIR: I agree.

PROSPERO: You don't object?

POLONIOUSS: Nobody objects. It's what we've all thought should happen, ever since this morning.

PROSPERO: What about you, Yago?

YAGO: I agree completely.

PROSPERO: You're lying.

YAGO: Not at all. If only you literary critics would realise that I'm not all bad!

PROSPERO: Edmon - what do you think? Wake up! (he slaps him) This is no time to sleep.

EDMON: What's happening? Where am I?

PROSPERO: I am Prospero, and I'm talking to you.

EDMON: Prospero? Oh God, forgive me.... (he faints again)

KING LIR: Let's take that as a "Yes". So - total agreement.

PROSPERO:	It's all very strange. I've been planning this scene for twenty years.... and it wasn't supposed to be at all like this.
ARYEL:	Captain...
PROSPERO:	Don't you talk to me! I'll deal with you later.
FERDJINAN:	You've forgotten about me. I don't agree.
PROSPERO:	I don't think that's allowed.
FERDJINAN:	I'm not one of your machines - you can't programme me to do what you want.
PROSPERO:	Do you know who you're talking to?
FERDJINAN:	I'm sorry to say I do. I used to hear about the great King Prospero, the philosopher-king. But all I see is another manipulator - just like Yago.
YAGO:	Not again! Aren't I allowed to change?
FERDJINAN:	I'm sorry, Yago - of course you can change. The whole world changes all the time. That's what you have to understand, Prospero. Perhaps your logic had some sort of value once. But the wind has changed. We don't believe in anyone's privileges any more.
PROSPERO:	Oh, really?
FERDJINAN:	You claim privileges for yourself. You say you're going to pass them on to your children and your children's children. But forget it. You want me to marry your daughter so that she becomes Queen: well, I'm telling you that I don't want it, I can't do it, and I don't agree to it. Anyway - I'm already engaged.
PROSPERO:	Engaged?
FERDJINAN:	Yes. To Aryel.
PROSPERO:	But Aryel -
FERDJINAN:	Yes, I know he doesn't have a sex. The whole point of me marrying your daughter was to breed an heir, but nobody's checked my breeding potential.
KING LIR:	What's the matter with it?
FERDJINAN:	Father, you remember that car accident I was in? Modern medicine may have saved my life, and plastic surgery given me back my face and most of my body - but not the bit that matters to you. I'm impotent, Dad. Sexual pleasure means nothing to me. In Aryel, I've found a genuine partner. That's all. Oh - you'll call it perverted, but to me this is what's normal.
PROSPERO:	So who succeeds to the throne?

FERDJINAN: Sort it out with my father. I'm really not interested in power.

KING LIR: What about you, Prospero?

PROSPERO: You must be joking.

KING LIR: Then what am I supposed to do with my throne?

PROSPERO: And what am I supposed to do with my daughter?

(Kordelia and Kalibann enter together)

KORDELIA: Is there some sort of problem, Dad?

PROSPERO: Kordelia.... Everything's gone wrong. I wanted you to get married to Ferdjinan, and he said no. I wanted you to be Queen.

KING LIR: That's it! Let's make your daughter Queen!

POLONIOUSS: What a brilliant idea! It's terribly fashionable to have a woman in charge. I second the motion.

KORDELIA: They've all gone mad.

PROSPERO: Now all we have to do is find a king or prince who's unmarried or widowed.

KORDELIA: You're off again! What about me? My feelings - what I want.

PROSPERO: What do you mean, Kordelia? You're a princess. That makes you special - and different.

FERDJINAN: He'll never learn.

KORDELIA: I can't get married.

KING LIR: Don't tell me you've had an accident as well.

KORDELIA: No - I chose. I chose Kalibann.

PROSPERO: (He can't control himself.) What?! This half-bred bat-

KORDELIA: Shut it, Dad! If you say that word, I'll never speak to you again.

PROSPERO: But, Kordelia - what about your future? It's decreed that you should be a great Queen and rule an Empire. You can't just spit on it.

KORDELIA: Who's supposed to have decreed this?

PROSPERO: Destiny.

KORDELIA: So Destiny wrote Destiny.....

PROSPERO:	This is impossible! You can't marry Kalibann.
KORDELIA:	Why not?
PROSPERO:	Isn't it obvious? He doesn't have royal blood.
KORDELIA:	He has human blood. That's enough for me. We really aren't interested in your power politics. We want to live according to what we feel.
PROSPERO:	Feelings! There's the root of the problem. Everybody's talking about their feelings! But you're ignoring the realities.
KORDELIA:	What reality is left? Since this morning no-one has had any idea of what was real and what was a dream. Dreams have become realities, and realities dreams. Fiction has taken the place of fact, and art is battling with life. There's a new form of reality struggling to be born. You've got to accept it, Father.

(Silence)

FERDJINAN:	Prospero; I'm sorry I spoke so harshly to you.
PROSPERO:	Aryel, come here. Why did you betray me?
ARYEL:	I have never betrayed you, Captain. I told you that something in my programming felt peculiar. Maybe something malfunctioning in my system. But, Captain - I'm happy as I am. I've not betrayed you: I've simply followed a programme which I couldn't control. Don't hold it against me.
PROSPERO:	How did I go so wrong?
KORDELIA:	I told you - things have changed. A victim can turn into an aggressor.
PROSPERO:	Meaning?
ARYEL:	Captain, nobody can deny that they did you wrong. You were quite right to look for justice but -
PROSPERO:	But what?
KORDELIA:	But, quite without meaning to, you got blinded by your own power, and stopped being able to tell the difference between justice and revenge.
KALIBANN:	Mr. Prospero.
PROSPERO:	What do you want?
KALIBANN:	You promised me my freedom. Since then I've come to understand exactly what that means. Can I ask you to keep your word?
PROSPERO:	Yes, yes.

KALIBANN: I am free then?

PROSPERO: You're free.

KALIBANN: Then I have the honour of asking you for your daughter's hand in marriage.

PROSPERO: You'll have the honour of my fist in your mouth!

KORDELIA: Father! You've got to accept this!

PROSPERO: Why?

KORDELIA: Because I'm pregnant!

PROSPERO: Oh - Toufann swallow me up! Just do what you want!

(Prospero starts to leave. Everyone else runs after him to stop him leaving.)

KING LIR: Prospero - this is the way to solve our problem. Let them get married. We can make Kalibann King. It's the only way.

PROSPERO: Kalibann?

POLONIOUSS: It's a wonderful idea!

PROSPERO: You think so?

KORDELIA: Father, who's your best student?

(Silence)

                 Who is the father of your grand-child?

(Silence)

                 Who is the only person capable of continuing your work?

PROSPERO: All right, I agree, but...

(Kordelia is hugging him)

SAILOR: Hey, everybody! We've all forgotten the tidal wave!

PROSPERO: Oh no - Aryel, Kalibann, come quickly! We need to stop the projection!

(Prospero, Kordelia, Aryel and Kalibann go. Darkness. Strange sounds and music - coloured lights and moving silhouettes. When the light returns to normal, everything is calm. The ship is anchored in a quiet sea.)

KING LIR:	This morning, I thought it was all over. But now - just look! The strange has become the normal.
FERDJINAN:	And the normal has become the strange. It's hard to think that all this happened in a single day. One era was just switched off, and a new age was born. Aryel's right - this is a magical island - like a womb. Everything is made ready here; new life ready to be sent out into a new world.
POLONIOUSS:	And if you look closely, you can see that the new is at once more powerful and more beautiful than the old. Lir - it's time for you and I to rest. The young can move life forward in their own way.

(Prospero, Aryel, Kordelia and Kalibann come back.)

PROSPERO:	It's safe now. I've dismantled everything. In a little while my island will vanish. It's done its job: it made all of us see our mistakes, and it's given birth to a new sort of destiny. The ship can cast off now.
SAILOR:	*(from offstage)* Let out the rope, weigh anchor!
PROSPERO:	You see this key[16]? This key switches off all my technology. It's the key to the heart of my power. If I throw this key into the sea, then all my magical power goes with it; the island will vanish and I'll be just like the rest of you. And that's what I'll do. (He throws the key into the sea.) My reign is over. Kordelia and Kalibann's reign has begun. My children - don't make the same mistakes your parents did.

(Shouts and disorder from offstage. The sailor runs in.)

SAILOR:	There's mutiny on board! Dammarro -
PROSPERO:	Damn everything, I say.
SAILOR:	Dammarro and Kaspalto have got the crew drunk. They're refusing to obey orders.
KALIBANN:	Why?
SAILOR:	Because they're opposed to your election, sir.
KORDELIA:	Call them in.

(The Sailor goes.)

FERDJINAN:	New King - new problems.
ARYEL:	Should I do something?

---

16   Apart from its obvious similarities to the speech which Shakespeare's Prospero makes about breaking his staff and drowning his book, this speech has very particular significance for a Mauritian audience. Sir Seewoosagur Ramgoolam (1900-85), known as "the father of the nation", was the leading campaigner for Mauritian independence, and the first Prime Minister of the independent state. He suffered his only political defeat in 1982, when he was ousted by the more radically socialist MMM of Anerood Jugnauth. Ramgoolam became the Governor-General, until his death in 1985. Ramgoolam's son Navin has since become leader of the Labour Party and Prime Minister. The symbol of Ramgoolam's Labour Party is the Red Key.

FERDJINAN: No, Aryel. Don't steal some-one else's thunder.

(The Sailor comes back, with Kaspalto, Dammarro and the ship's crew.)

KALIBANN: Now, Kaspalto, tell me your demands.

DAMMARRO: We are making....

KALIBANN: Who's the leader? Kaspalto or Dammarro?

KASPALTO &
DAMMARRO: Me.

KALIBANN: You need to decide who the leader is.

KASPALTO &
DAMMARRO: Both of us.

KALIBANN: So - tell me.

KASPALTO: You tell him, Dammarro man.

DAMMARRO: Oh my goodness no. You be telling him yourself.

KASPALTO: We doesn't want you as King, man. I says I should be-

DAMMARRO: No! It's me. You are usurping my rightful place...

KORDELIA: Kaspalto, Dammarro - listen to me. You've arrived on the scene too late. The story's finishing. Can't you see that?

DAMMARRO: What of us? Do you think we are nothing but the couch potatoes? If you can make that silly fellow King - then why not us? We are the children of the country; but everyone is behaving as if we do not exist.

ARYEL: Don't worry. I'll talk to the boss. I'll get him to write a new story. One where you become king.

KASPALTO &
DAMMARRO: In that case, we agree.

KALIBANN: Cast off, then!

The End

Dev Virahsawmy was born in Mauritius in 1942. His schooling was in Mauritius, and he attended the University of Edinburgh. His dissertation was called *Towards a Revaluation of Mauritian Creole*, a theme which has continued in all his subsequent work. Dev is a passionate campaigner for the establishment of Creole (or, his preferred term, Morisien) as the national language of Mauritius: a language of literature, culture and government, as well as daily life. From 1966 to 1987, Dev was actively involved in Mauritian politics. Since then, he has concentrated on writing in Morisien. Plays include the celebrated (and long-banned) *Li* (Winner 11th Concours de Radio-France International 1981), *Abs Lemanifik*, *Zeneral Makbef*, *Toufann*, *Petal ek Pikan* and *Kayse Ba*. Translations and adaptations include *Trazedji Makbess* (Macbeth), *Enn Ta Senn Dan Vid* (Much Ado About Nothing), *Zil Sezar* (Julius Caesar), *Galileo Gonaz* (Life of Galileo), *Tartchif Froder* (Le Tartuffe) and *Zozef* (Joseph and the Amazing Technicolour Dreamcoat). His recent play, *Sir Toby*, was written in response to Border Crossings' production of *Twelfth Night* in Mauritius. Dev lives in Rose-Hill, Mauritius, with his wife Loga and his daughters Saskia and Anushka.

Nisha Walling was born in Mauritius, and studied painting at Santiniketan in India. She played Lady Macbeth in Michael Walling's production in Mauritius in 1997. Since coming to England, she has appeared (under her acting name Nisha Dassyne) in *Mappa Mundi* for Border Crossings, *Nana's Nightingale* (Royal Theatre, Northampton) and *Around the World in Eighty Days* (Proteus). She lives in London with her husband Michael and their children Hari and Amba.

Michael Walling is Artistic Director of Border Crossings. He has directed numerous productions across four continents, winning awards for *Two Gentlemen of Verona* in the US and *Paul & Virginie* in Mauritius.

Border Crossings productions include: *The Dilemma of a Ghost* (UK tour; co-produced with National Theatre of Ghana), *Dis-Orientations* (Riverside Studios, London; co-produced with Shanghai Yue Opera Company), *Uniforms & Hoodies* (Patti Smith's Meltdown at the Royal Festival Hall), *Bullie's House* (UK tour and Riverside Studios; co-produced with Jiriki Management, Australia; Critics Choice in Time Out and Metro), *Orientations* (UK tours and Oval House, London; co-produced with Yaksha Degula, India), *Double Tongue* (by Brian Woolland; UK tour & tour of Hungary), *Mappa Mundi* (UK tours and Tamaulipas International Festival, Mexico), *Toufann* (London), *Twelfth Night* (tours of UK, Mauritius, Seychelles & Zimbabwe for the British Council), *Bravely Fought the Queen* (UK tour), *Departures / Arrivals* (UK tour) and *Fool for Love* (London).

Work as a director elsewhere includes: *Die Zauberflöte* (Spain), *Macbeth* (Mauritius), *The Tempest* (India), *Attempts on Her Life*, *Victory*, *Hard Times*, *The Art of Success*, *Don Giovanni*, *Così fan Tutte*, *The Marriage of Figaro* (all UK), *Romeo and Juliet* (USA), *The Great God Brown*, *Beardsley*, *Play with Cocaine*, *Spokesong*, *Sir Thomas More* (all UK). Michael directed the ENO's acclaimed semi-stagings of *The Ring* at the Coliseum and the Barbican, the Greek National Opera's *Nixon in China* (with Peter Sellars) and (with Phyllida Lloyd) *The Handmaid's Tale* for Canadian Opera Company.

Michael has published extensively on theatre and related subjects. Most recently, he has written a chapter for a new book on the plays of Mahesh Dattani, and has edited Border Crossings' book *Theatre and Slavery: Ghosts at the Crossroads*.

Plans include: *A Midsummer Night's Dream* (Lake Tahoe Shakespeare Festival, USA), and a Chinese tour of *Dis-Orientations*, including the Shanghai International Festival. Michael is also director of the *Origins* Festival of First Nations Theatre, in which Border Crossings is a co-producer.